The Hunter's Horn

Gaie Vickers

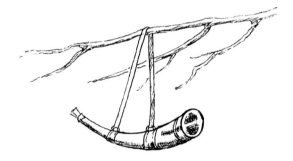

George Mann Publications

A CIP catalogue record for this book
is available from the British Library

ISBN 9780955241536

George Mann Publications

Contents

~ Dedicated to ~

Jessie Roberts (née Gell),
my paternal grandmother
whose short life,
so starkly remembered
in a dusty cemetery in Pakistan,
deserves a deeper commemoration.

Introduction

This book is a compilation of poems that include some I published in 1988. The reason for the title becomes clear when I explain that, for me, the word 'inspiration' holds the evocative image of a crystal horn blown through the dark forests of the mind. In the clear moonlight the hunter raises the horn to his lips ~ a clarion call, echoing, reverberating through the woods, across the countryside. The quarry leaps ahead ~ white and silver flashing through the trees ~ darting, evading, but, sometimes, captured, held.

The impulse to write poetry stemmed from a specific event: somewhere between the ages of thirteen or fourteen, I fell down a flight of steps and fractured the base of my skull. This resulted in several weeks lying prone in a darkened room and it was during this period that I first started putting pen to paper. Poetry, not prose, seemed the only way to fulfil this urge, being paradoxically, more concise and yet more open to description and flights of imagination. Ever since then I have been fascinated by 'logos': that most powerful of words that incorporates the vibration of words, the sound of words, the juxtaposition of words, the homecoming of words, by which I mean that inspired arrangement of metre and words that gives a thought its own unique form. For me every deep emotion, every memorable experience, every unusual thought needs to be concretised in some poetic shape or other. Sometimes a poem will come to me entire and whole ~ such as the *W.R.A.C's Lament* which was 'written' whilst I was busy hoovering! Similarly, *Europa*, began and completed itself whilst cooking supper. Usually, however, it is the first three or four lines which are the inspiration. The words sound loud and clear in my head and I continue from there. However much I am stirred by an event if those lines don't write themselves I know it is pretty welt useless going on. I subscribe to John Keats' theory that unless verse falls as naturally as leaves from a tree it is better not to attempt to write at all. I am therefore rather a lazy writer and spend far too little time on editing and tidying up. 'What you see is what you get' as they say, and once the words have appeared and been consigned to paper I find it difficult to be interested in them anymore.

Someone recently asked me whether I could say how my poems had evolved, if at all, over the years. It's a very difficult question to answer. On impulse, I would say that I have now established my own voice. The influence of Keats, Yeats and T. S. Eliot are all too obvious in the early poems; in fact the opening poem, written to a wonderful nun, Mother Wilson, who taught English at the Sacred Heart Convent I attended in Tunbridge Wells, is pure Yeats, but I include it because I owe her an enormous debt of gratitude for the love and appreciation of all things literary which she awoke in me. The traces of other poets are obvious, but, so what? I was only 14 or so, and other people's words whirled and swirled in my mind. I was awash with them, so small wonder that they turned up every now and then. In fact I once sat outside in the pouring rain willing myself to get consumption if only I could write like Keats! Needless to say, I never got the consumption and failed to write like Keats. I suppose I could say that over the years the almost painful intensity of experience has mellowed somewhat and that, maybe, I am calmer, wiser. What has not changed, however, is that sense of mystic wonder I experienced as I lay beneath the flowering cherries in our garden recovering from my concussion: an overpowering sense of beauty, love and interconnectedness with all things. That absolute resonance and all-encompassing presence of God (without any sense of formal religion) has always been the prime mover behind my writing and that 'other world' remains close and important to me.

Perhaps three poems need explaining. In each case they arose violently and emotionally within me and were written within about ten minutes of the event. The first one is *Agnus Dei*. This was a very symbolic photograph in the Daily Telegraph, taken the week after 9/11, showing a small boy of about three years old running across a field carrying three crosses in his arms in order for them to be planted among 3,000 others commemorating all those who lost their lives in the Twin Towers. The second, also in the Daily Telegraph, was a heart rending photograph of the young Arab boy, Ali Ishmael Abbas, who lost both his arms and was severely burnt when a bomb dropped on Bhagdad. The photograph literally stopped me in my tracks and I burst into tears at the sight of such terrible meaningless tragedy. The angle of the arm stumps was such that, at the first glance I thought he was laid out as for crucifixion. Thankfully it was not so, and in the strange way of the world, all the media attention meant that young Ali went on to have the best medical help possible and state of the art prosthesis. The third poem, *His Death by Hanging,* commemorates a more recent event and one, which as I heard it on the early morning news made me cry out silently, *No!* It felt so wrong, though I know there are many who will disagree.

I have been very lucky throughout my life to have had spiritual teachers, mentors and friends whose inspiration and input has opened windows on to many strange, wonderful and varied lands. I am so grateful, so indebted, to all of them for what they have led me to view and experience. Without them my life would have been considerably poorer ~ diminished, in fact ~ and the poems in this book would have been far fewer. We live in such a wonderful world but we need to see through the eyes of others as well as our own to fully appreciate its beauty. We need to be touched by the joys and sadnesses of others, as well as our own, to fully experience what it is to be alive. I am also enormously indebted and grateful to George Mann for his advice, skill and enthusiasm in printing this book; it would never have looked as beautiful as it does without his experienced input.

Someone once told me that I was a 'true poet', in that the true poet, regardless of his skill, status or success, has 'the heart of a child'. If that is so, then I hope I will remain that way and that the sense of wonder and beauty that has been so important in my life, will never, even in my second childhood, desert me.

The Burning Soul

I wrote my poems for you, because I loved,
O Woman of the burning soul.
The dawn of youth burnt bright and clear
That I might so give back to you
A little of the love infused
Into my wordless mind.
Now, suddenly, the magic's fled,
And all seems dead and grey;
O Woman of the burning soul
Give back that gift to me.

The Moment

Alone I stood on the windy hill,
Alone, and brave and free.
Above me sped the thunderous sky,
Around me lay the heathered moors,
Below me roared the sea.
I felt the brine upon my lips,
And, laughing, flung my arms in praise;
The world was mine; all power was mine,
And manhood stretched before my eyes
In an exultant blaze.
Then, suddenly, the winds grew cruel
And round my body flayed,
While swiftly flashing forth its rage
The sky came down to earth and found
A trembling boy ~ afraid.

Diminuendo

The burden bears too hard
Upon an untried soul,
All-failing, tiring soul
Treading such thorns.
The warm soft hand
No longer heals,
But, pointing, mocks
The flaming weals;
The arrow shaft
Deep-quivering strikes,
And poisoning, kills
Both love and faith.
Till fever-tossed
Unknown, unloved,
Hurled in the hell
Of blinding hate
Is left the heart ~
Poignant, pensive
Pale-lipped, still
Hovering, trembling
Homeless waif,
Love shadows yet
The heart once chaste.
Unheard the horn,
Unknown the dove,
Whose purging flames,
A people's grace,
Come sweeter, softer
In their love.

Yet, somewhere hid
The rose's heart
Crystal clear
Mantles love;
Hushing ~ fear-free,
Calming, soothing,
Till fear and sorrow
Flee the dark
To see the morrow
Dew-kissed wake,
And live and laugh.

Crescendo

Air-elusiveness, thistle-down uncaught;
Air-free, wind-free, far-flying thought.
Water-clear, sin-free
Heaven-bound soul.
Wild rose, frail rose
Love-pulsing heart.
Warm hands, soft hands
Healing each part.
Winged thought, not tamed thought
Following the stars,
Creating with purport
Life in the flowers
Grace in a shower ...
Yet I am locked out
For I cannot rise
And make my thought dance
With the soft-dimpled skies.
The wrinkled dawn,
The rose's thorn,
The fearful dark
And empty laugh,
With weaving fingers
Catch and bind
Frail human-kind.
Still, few have flown far
Have torn loose those threads
Of listlessly waiting,
Impatiently hurrying
Life of the dead ...

To follow, to follow
Fresh dew-webbed at morn
The wild clear horn,
Echoing, beckoning,
Haunting, alluring, still
Never caught trail
Of symphonious thought;
In realms were unwrought
Music comes flowering,
Cascading, showering ~
Happiness found,
Or lost?

Books

I entered in; and like a bird
That only knew the caging bars,
I soared into a truth of words;
Self was distilled, the very jars
That shook my spirit's mortal life
Were smoothed away; the very I
Was liberated from the strife
Of time and place, and I could fly
Into a world another shaped;
But I could view with different eyes,
But I could see ~ where others gaped
The wrong side of the looking glass ~
A new life, not a new escape,
Vital, throbbing, not the farce
Of oneness that we seek to trace
This side of the prison wall.
But transcending time and place
And separateness, its haunting call
A magic spell, setting free
Earthbound man to the firmanent
Of the spirit, that he may see
From afar the living moment,
From afar a truth's new light.
And though the spell of art must break
And I return from my wild flight,
Yet still the memory, like a wake
Ever widening down the years,
Holds the knowledge of the oneness,
Of the living with the dead,
Through imprisonments and fears.
And then it must but feel compassion
Following where the spirit led.

Sonnet on the Coronation

School Prize

Like a swan cresting o'er the wave
And piercing through the waters with the whiteness
Of its breast, leaving in its brightness
A shimmering, widening wake the sun may lave
With golden, gleaming ripples ∼ so down the nave
In their queen's wake, the very gliding lightness
Of their step, like some dream of sightless
Nights, passed the train beauteous and grave.
While rising from their misty tombs, those few
Who ruled and fought for their loved motherland:
Great kings and poets born of English air,
Triumphant claimed our noble queen anew;
Whilst loyal subjects prayed on either hand ∼
Young of heart ∼ in answer to her prayer.

The Annunciation

Wonderous, hovering, soft he came
Calling oft the Virgin's name,
"Hail, Mary full of grace".
The Voice, all hidden,
Waiting, list.
The world, all trembling,
Wonder wist.
It lay not in the 'yes' or 'no',
It lay not in the eyes or lips,
But in a heart, God-humbled, low,
It lay, love-bounded,
Every part in willingness
To God's word given ~
Exulting, flute-like
Voices rang;
Soaring, quivering
Rising upwards.
Softer, falling
Through the arches,
Through the golden trailing clouds.

Stella Maris! Praying soul
What saw you then
With head low bowed,
And heart o'erflowing
In its love?
The sudden knowledge of creation
To be nourished, succoured, loved.
The sudden knowledge of some mission
Taking being from above.
A baby fair,
All sin-free, dear,
Pure as the soft snow
Falling down ~
Adoration of the lowly,

14

Humble, meek and yet most great.
Love-shining eyes,
Gnarled, trembling hands,
Prayer-fixed they kneel
In homage meet ~
Great ones born of noble birth
Thus adoring bow their heads,
Peerless riches freely offer
From the love that stirs their hearts.

O Rosa Mystica! Sorrowing love!
The thorn prick, the phantasmous dream
Stretch out their hands to bind your soul
Away from God.

The Mother's heart
Holds still a fear,
Her Son, Her Son
Why must he die?
High hangs he there
For mankind's sake.
O, cruel wood
To bear him so!
O, thoughtless man
That did sin so!
Yet after woe
In some small part
There is a joy
To mend the heart ~
God's will is done
What need we fear?

The Virgin raised her eyes,
Once bowed her head,
And rose with joy
At God's great word ~
Now bound eternally
The Rose and the Love are one.

The Contemplative

Amid the flux of consciousness I moved,
Unmoved, invulnerable and with a stillness
Born of contemplation; for I loved
The cell of inmost thought, whitewashed and clean,
And, seeking the prime mover of mankind,
From there I watched their hurryings unseen.
Poor fools! What endless fooleries they wean
Their childhoods soul upon that it should grow
Like flowers beneath the stone, small, twisted so.

They have not found that lightness of the soul,
That sudden flash of vision now and then
That blinds the very spirit in the bowl
Of whirling life, and from the nursery pen
Of this world's ways releases all. These are
The spurned rewards of prolonged meditation.
Abstract, and no man seeks to search afar
What he can think to find, for consolation,
In material things; he cannot know
The stillness of the spirit in the world
That's fashioned by the discipline of quiet,
A territory wherein the spirit's furled
And crinkled corners may at last fly free.
A harp that's purely strung and sounds true notes,
A perfect tension so that man may see
And hear the world around as one may hear
The distant splashing of a waterfall,
So permanent that it shall cease to bear

Upon the senses though it still must fall;
A quiet retiring place where the harsh winds
Of high ambition, lust and fear may not
Disturb, nor yet can their chill fingers bind
And creep around the heart. Action shall rot
And perish in the waves of time, but thought
Must live and conquer in the outer space
Of meditation; daydreams cheaply bought
As contemplation shall wither in the face
Of truth; it is the inward stillness
Of perfect balance, not indifference,
That makes invulnerable, with quietness
The thinking man. The whole significance
Of life lies in the contemplation of a truth,
Lies in a sudden bursting knowledge
That man must kneel in second place and not aloof
Seek to be first, that he must dare to know
What others fear through some fear of themselves.

The Rebel

Rebel in the darkly narrow time
Of birth and death; subject to the
Mutability of this and that; I seek,
Unknowing, for the sudden flash
Forked down the soul. Rebirth
From dark to lightness, tearing out
The towering cumulus amassed
Within the brain. Defying whispered
Tensions till the scaffold falls to crush
The nightmare world below ~
Till suddenly the empty cry is heard,
And answered, in the loneliness of space.

Rosa Mystica!

Triolet

Rosa Mystica! White criimsoned red,
Cross-watching, sorrowing over the night,
Loving and praying till dawning of light,
Kissing the crosswood where a Son bled.
Chaste and untouched, from thee sin has fled
Unable to wrong in thy grace-filling sight.
Rosa Mystica! White crimsoned red,
Give me, oh, give me the love for all shed,
Give me your patience, your strength and your
    might,
Give me your gentleness, purity-white.
To thee do I pray with a soul all sin-led,
Rosa Mystica!, white crimsoned red.

Sonnet

There is glory in our youth. To be
Alive and free, accepting what is now
And seeking not before or after; to see
Life as a lovely wild thing, and know
That there is laughter in the wind and rain
And love in every moment, every hour.
Alone on starlit nights to cry again,
"Life is here, is now, lies in the flower,
Leaf and pool of light, unchanged and free".
And take the challenge, laughing, proud and strong,
Knowing not fear nor what it is to flee,
But glorying only in life's passionate song ~
And the glories of this youth will fill our day
When we are tired and faded, old and grey.

Sonnet

If there is sorrow equal to the love,
If there is pain to equal all the joy ~
Then let it come ~ and let the world employ
Its mind to our destruction ~ Cast the glove
Before our feet and clip the wingèd dove;
Spit in our eyes. Is love a child's toy
That mortal things by threatening, destroy,
And in destroying break the faith above?

But love and all the glory we have known
The laughter and the tears ~ how can they die?
Within our fading memories shall we live,
Blind to the ways we walk, but fuller grown
In strength of spirit; till with a little sigh
The body dies, and soul joins soul to give.

Sonnet

When you and I lie empty, grave and cold,
Senseless to warmth of touch, caress of hair,
Blind to the streaming sun, the clear crisp air
That once we breathed and gloried in of old;
When only a wordless stone stands to unfold
The passion of our life, as young and fair
We found the whole world to ourselves, and where
We roamed love followed blazing a trail of gold ~
Does it not seem strange when we have gone
That love must shine through other eyes and speak
Through other lips, that what we know by others
Is also known, and stars that shone
For us shine for them too? And yet how bleak
Compared to ours, must their love be, poor lovers!

After Rupert Brooke?

Remember that day? How breathless and hand-in-hand
We flung ourselves down on the heathered ground, and the
    thrill
Of being alive and ourselves shattered the still
Passiveness of the day, till even the sands
Wrinkled far below, became intimate, warm and
At one with us ~ how we lay back and drank our fill
Of that perfectness ~ let the sun blaze down until
Our spirits lay eased and before us eternity spanned?

Remember that day? How bitterly I cried,
"Why all things ~ even the greatest ~ change in the end;
While Truth's unattainable; love is fickle and fast."
And gazing down at the sea you softly replied,
"This will not change ~ the moment when two souls lend
The other comfort and ease ~ this will keep to the last".

Ungrateful Guest

You do not know how careless words can smart.
How jokes can pierce like shattered shards.
How these can make a trustful loving heart,
Bleed ceaselessly ~ and then turn cold and hard.

But when one day you turn to warm your hands
Before the glowing fire, ungrateful guest,
Only an empty, staring grate will stand,
Only an empty room will echo back your jests.

Will Time Destroy

Will time destroy us, slipping through our hands?
Seeping through our youth like some decay,
Weaving small contempts like iron bands
Around the once too burning, passionate day?

Will time destroy us, darkening the line
Of life, of love, draining warmth away,
Binding the unbounded with a fine
Clear spider's web, turning flesh to clay?

Will time destroy us in the dark of night
When we may turn for touch or flash of eye,
And find an empty ghost, a soul in flight
When we are dust, and can no longer sigh?

Dislike of Drawing Room Farce

Hypocrisy on a sofa; the smiling mask
Turned mutely through the rise and fall of voices,
That, with a vague hysteria attempt
To find some reason for communication.
Lonely eye reflects in lonely eye,
And emptiness is drowned in glass and laugh.
Guilt is hidden; barriers are raised,
Protective foil to hide the jagged ends
Of unaccepted thoughts, defeated aims;
While, as an iron band convention holds
The sudden rents where too much soul is seen,
Ensures that no-one may reveal their lonely
Living hell nor ask for sympathy ...
... The glasses drained, wide-eyed and fever bright,
They think they've found a reason to their life,
The answer hangs, and mocking tantalises
All too eager hands that from the babel
Reach with hungry fingers supplicating,
Blind to the euphoric haze that wreathes
And swirls around them in a cruel delight.
Till, suddenly, the door slams ~ in the cold
That momentary insight fades away ~
Collars up, they turn their heads aside,
Afraid of fear, of others, of themselves.

On having seen Delacroix's Picture

'The Entry of the Crusaders into Jerusalem'

Oh, how we had dreamed of the splendour,
 the glory, the praise.
How we mercilessly laughed like the giants as we
swept through the land,
And thrilled to the sound of the clash of the blade
 and the blaze
Of the miles behind. And the might and the
 strength of the hand
Plunging the sword seemed filled with the might of ten,
As onwards and onwards we rode, powerful and glorious;
Till high on the hill the red crescent sank and our men
Raised the gold lion to its height, and we entered
 victorious.
But just as we crested the rise of the hill there fell
A quietness around us; a woman's low sob pierced the
 hour
Of our triumph; it seemed that suddenly no man could tell
His reason for being; our victory turned bitter and sour.
As the smoke from the slow-dying city blackened the
 skies,
As bewildered and mazed in our hearts, the light left our
 eyes.

Pop Death

(Daily Telegraph competition, 1973)

Crazed like the Maenaeds,
Yearly at the dionysian rite,
They seek the young king
High upon his dais;
Dare to touch his youth,
His temporal godhead;
And moving on a frenzied tide,
Their shining, upturned faces
Are glazed with hidden, deep desires,
Which trapped in teenage innocence
Are now denied the ritual of death;
The darkened hall mere substitute
For moonlit woods and hills
That ring with breathless laughter
And final, dizzying sleep.
The wave of high hysteria
Crescendos to a tumbling peak,
And though their idol,
Just remote from predatory,
Grasping hands, still stands
Unscathed, the ugly god
Of their massed selves
Demands a sacrifice;

Till felled beneath the press
And frenzied push of bodies
The victim lies ~
Hair splayed out like summer rain,
Soft body quiet and still,
Youth spent, heart bruised,
Bones broken in the mindless crush ~
And the dark god smiles,
For he alone it seems
Remembers through the depths of time
The yearly ritual ending in a death;
Again, again enacting through the scene
To think ourselves sophisticated, new,
Forgetting what we were, or when,
Unmindful of the laws of fate
Upon the gross presumption made by men.

Amulet (of Kiliphi)

Sickle sail drawn on an azure sky,
Wide-winging through the deep, curled pelt of sea;
A whispered thought, a faint remembered sigh,
That spirit-like between these lonely lands,
Thrust upwards from a sea-god's mighty wrath,
May weave, with shining, many coloured strands,
An amulet of peace; spun hour by hour
With threads of happiness, made gold with sun,
Musk-scented with the crush of herb and flower,
And studded with a press of silver stars.
Libations from a never empty cup;
A panacea of golden liquid spilled,
Caught in the winds, and flung afar
To calm Poseidon's deep. A heart of truth
Still seeking, searching down the moon's white wake
The mightiness of gods. To keep as proof
That one small moment bound enduringly
Calm-healing through the coldness of the dawn,
Still-held within an amulet of peace.

First Thoughts on Yoga

In layers, discovering, unfolding, growing,
Reaching to a new world's light and breath,
To where the silent empty pool reflects
Another face caught from a different time,
That echoing half remembered thoughts and dreams,
Quickens the senses, opens out the mind,
As to a golden summer warmth of sun.
Till what was once a withered, wintered thought
Stirs with an unused pulse, awake, aware,
And reaching through the darkened earth of life
Bursts open to reveal the many petalled
Lotus bloom of calm tranquillity;
The dazzling light of freedom within self
The perfect circling of an endless truth.

The Room

We should remember this little room,
Pale flaky walls a dusty sun lays bare,
Tumbled blankets, rough and warm, the smell
Of tenderness, all wrapped for one sharp moment
In an air of love and held within
A drop of time; a womb-world, unassailable
In day or place, forgotten by the mind;
A dividend of love for two to share,
And miser-like set by a hoard for distant memories.
Yes, we should remember this little room, but we forget
That sadness lies in the creeping of time,
When two are no longer one;
When one heart flies and the other must hold
The tears of remembering.

Autumn

Will autumn always be like this?
Seared gold across a crystal sky
And aching with a summer's memories.
A final ecstacy in passion flung
Through woods and fields, kaleidoscope
Of drifting leaves, and hazy hills
Caught in the running edges of the sky.

Will autumn always be like this?
Bleeding, dying on the ground,
So glorious, so passionate, and yet
Still slowly dying, every hue
Defying winter and the grey of death
With golden laughter rustled on the air
And quivered like a lost soul through the leaves.

Will autumn always be like this?
Clutching at my heart with memories,
Bleeding, dying at my feet, a lingering smile
Strewn across the countryside,
Leaving me sad and helplessly
Staring at death caught in a few brown leaves.

Winter Death

Free, the small bird through her green wood flew,
Content with twig and shimmer of leaf,
Bright berries and the blue of days;
Her song, unnoticed, held a gaiety
That could not know the depth of pain,
Her small life filled and busy with the task
Of living; till, unheralded,
With flash of fiery red and trailing gold,
Shattering the safety of her wood,
The Bird of Paradise beside her flew,
Trembled his shimmering gold and red,
And captured her small but busy life,
The innocence deep in her heart.

And so the summer passed;
Filled with the splendour of this glorious bird,
She followed where he flew,
Wood no longer world enough
But far across the mellowing fields
Into the dying of the sky,
Watching the world from green to gold
Shiver on a winter's edge;
The Bird of Paradise, his feathers fluffed,
Cried his soft goodbyes with promises
And flew away ...
The wood grew quiet
And fainter still the small bird's song,
His promises like distant hopes
No longer warmed her chilling heart,
For how could he in all his grandeur know
The cruel of winter ending in a death
And final flurry of a small brown wing?

Waiting

Does earth in winter waiting know this pain?
Sterile land and barren trees,
My heart is slowly oozing life,
Red colour of a fallen leaf
Crumpled on the ground.

Does night in darkness waiting feel the same?
Before the moon ascends the studded sky,
My darkling heart in shadows beating
Frail wings that hold the running hours,
And endless pain of time.

Does wind still whisper hope through dying trees,
Does night still know full well the promise made?
Must lovers through their own life thread,
Deep passion-carved, these tiny deaths?
Like earth and sky keep waiting hearts,
And know that what is dearly loved
Must surely live again, and on,
Through many seasons endlessly.

Outcast

And what of the you and I
Drowned in the naked moment
Of a glance?
Will we survive
As the tiny bell
Of our leprosy
Hurries its willing way
Across the bridge?
For now, with the heart laid bare
All safety's gone,
And thought is tender
Turned to dreams.
Except we ring our minds
With fortressing of cult and custom
There lies no real defence,
And so it seems
That eyes must close and senses reel
As we drown in the depths of a glance.

Perseus

Perseus with his Gorgon's head,
Warding off the curious eye,
Logic and a secret brought
To the rambling mind of man.
But discovered all too late
The secret of divinity,
Fell beneath his awful fate,
The death mask of virginity.

Parry the Fates

Parry the Fates, and then let them decide
When the glance took focus
And the wish became a deed.
Whether we, beneath the trees
Vaulting their green-domed
Ecstasy towards the sky,
Are blessed with merely human luck,
Enacting once again
The dionsyian rite
With signs and kisses
And the sudden loss of words.
Or, whether by defiance
Of an inauspicious start,
We earn the angry envy of the gods
And cripple our frail selves
Upon a dark-eyed hate,
So to be branded with
A short loves life.

Rapport

Unseen the hand that softly draws
A quivering from the ten string harp;
Completeness of music through the still,
Dark, waiting halls, and
The sudden mind allied to that
Strange possible ghost is strung
As taut aware and knows
Music rapt and rare as any.

Towers and turrets are there many
Within the minds of men,
And all too rarely shared
Their hidden, lonely rooms.
Here lies no false pretence,
The harp should quiver,
You should find
Within my moated, castled mind
Like thoughts and words
In tumbled disarray,
Waiting for the ordered form
That makes perfection
Of the living thing.

The white knight on his timeless search;
The tall tower built without a door;
The burning grail shines rich and fierce
And all the while there swoops and soars
Through empty, still and waiting halls
That ghostly music rapt and rare.

Had There Been Time

Had there been time would 'like' have turned to 'love'?
Or would reiteration maim and spoil
This moment hanging like a sword
Steel bright between us? The subtle point
When 'almost' becomes fact, the tremulous
Opening of flowers to the sun,
The no-man's land where now we stand
Lost on the brink of a dream,
Enraptured, captured, snared by time.
Or do we gain, foreseeing ecstacy,
And through our deprivation save
From hurt and death the fraility
That's love. How better far
Never to know the dying day but feel
The endless all-awareness of its birth.

Invocation

Measure of bodies, and litmus of the mind,
Makes two and two, but where disaster pends
Five is the number of the day;
Though seven still a heaven away
Waits wide and wary for the number nine
To signify an end to all this mime.
Invocation of these numbers still depends
On gods and godesses,
Belief in Fate but not in men.

Growing

That day we grew
From the once of you and I
To an endless now;
From a childhood myth of dream and mist
Where we clung by a harebell's breath
To the green, grass hill,
To a soft dissolvement
Caught in the gentle breeze,
And hung in the running edges of the sky;
From a moment made of poem and rhyme
To that strange point where no words are
The spaces grew
And made us infinite,
Till time and our beating hearts
Were stilled
To a perfect now.

Memory

Looking at your face
Now once more etched
Upon the dark horizons of my mind,
I know the memory lines
Were full perfection;
How else the true recall
With not one faltering stroke
To make the picture whole?
How else the deep remembered
Knowledge, held like a child
Within the womb, fed with
A heart's full mother love,
And born with the beating pulse
Of life to love and laughter?
How else the buttressed walls of time and space
Dissolved to nothingness,
And that strange, dark divide
United in awareness, and made whole
Within our dreaming, bonded selves?

Singapore University Forum

On the effects of the oil crisis in South-East Asia

Sitting here,
slightly tight ~
vodka-toniced ~
watching you
fiddling with
a nervous tie,
and listening to
impossible
oriental syllables
of English words;
wondering if oil
and Asia
really matter ~
I slightly giggle
(foolish bird
amongst the earnestness
of men)
tin cans and oil
rosy pictures of Malaya
seem bobbing
on an eddless tide
of economic
not to say political
factors
caught round Singapore.

from horn-rimmed
spectacles,
embarrassed choking
on the straws
in fizz-pop bottles,
to billion-dollared sheiks
and all external debts
I wander,
subject to
fragmented thoughts
impinging on
my seriousness,
wondering who,
in a thousand years ~ or less ~
will really care
the whys and whens
and whether
it wouldn't be better
if we all quite simply
returned
to the beginning
and scratched our energy
before the Fire God
with two
Yin and Yang
uncomplicated sticks.

Promises

Promises are funny things,
You trust so hard in them,
But sometimes,
Somehow,
They never happen;
And that is stranger still
Because you've always learnt
That Promises
MUST NOT BE BROKEN!
                    Yet it seems
That I am always sweeping up
The shining, tiny pieces
Of a broken promise;
Sometimes mine,
Sometimes someone else's.
They lie like shattered tears
Upon the ground;
And you feel the very earth
Would flood,
There are so many of them.

Lost Kitten

Half-past eleven;
I might have been asleep
Or even dreaming quietly of you,
And never heard your ring
Upon the bell,
Or seen the small, sad creature
Mewing in your hands.
Who would have thought
That life curled in a tiny ball
Of kitten, could ever breathe so small?
Or cry with such demand
Upon the world
His right to live?
Who would have thought
That we could watch
His every move with so much pride?
Or that days
Should whittle down
To listening for the plaintive cry,
Four-hourly feeds
With dropper tops
And endless love ...
And now you've gone away
This tiny thing of flesh and fur
Still needs me
Much as I need you.
I hold his mewing softness
To my cheek and think
How strange of love
To leave a kitten in my arms
In memory of you.

Dream Sequence

Hard in the cruel deep black of night,
You took our dream-child, newly born,
And flared the hidden depths with light
Of fire.
The soundless scream slow-motioned,
The charred remains like lenten ashes lay
With only the breeze to move and stir them.
"A child is woman's need for flattery", you said.
Hyperbole of words followed by
The treasonable paradox of silence
Changed into a bayonet sharp thust
As I lay floating in the cool,
Calm waters of the swimming pool.
The pale blue tinged to pink,
Dimly the thrusts from every side
Filmed, misted, blood-red, as my eyes
Fell softly closed beneath the waves.
But still you laughed out, loud and long,
Masked face implacable,
"The inner workings of the mind
Are mine alone, no man to take
The fortressed citadel, no woman to besiege
Audacious in the very act
The moated walls. Who needs a woman long?"
I heard the words still echoing,
Though water filled my ears, my eyes;
I could not die, only the burning pain
Remained, only the terrible, still
Slow-motioned scream rang through my soul,
And you, unpitying.

Parting

Sadness, as I recall,
Is the slim line of your back
Turned through the hurrying crowd
To wave a last good-bye.
And the hustling airport lounge
Becoming mist and tears
As your face fades,
For in my heart I know
The ticket is one way;
There is no return to love
Or even the tiny hope
Of seeing you again.
A thousand miles apart
I'll trace your memory
In poems and things,
Knowing that everyday
You'll grow a little fainter
In my mind, until
Even the aching sadness
Becomes a faint remembered
Song from long ago,
That somewhere in the morning,
Or even in the night,
The hot, dark city night,
I might softly sing,
Forgetful then of where it first began.

To John Keats

I wonder if you knew I loved you?
Endlessly we're told there is no past,
No future,
But an ever-changing consciousness
That runs within eternity;
My moon is sullied,
Twentieth century knowledge
Has smudged virginity
Across a sky no longer studded
Fierce with stars that hold a fate
In lofty splendour,
But rather finds it stirs and shakes
With man-made sound.
Suppose, within this time, that you had seen
A scrubby schoolgirl adolescent
Open your poems,
Tumble years away ...
Be born anew, lovely as a Naiad,
With her swift, pale-flowing form
Darting between the tumbling streams,
Soft, elusive, shy as dawn ~
And learn of love in beauty
Curved around the mind in gleams
Of sensuous light and languid dreams;
Know passion, silver-cupped,
And stars and moon rise high
Upon the velvet budding of the soul.

Find bitterness and pain,
Red upon white, the message shown,
And know, in youth,
Like autumn leaves soft rustling,
The whispering of death;
Till with what tenderness
Do schoolgirl-thin brown arms
Hold the pale and dying man
In that small, present, past and future,
Lonely room in Rome?
Take life like that
And you had never died,
But through our modern
Dull, polluted minds,
The hunter's horn is faintly heard,
Reborn eternally; kaleidoscope
Of brilliant, tumbling words
Opening up new sights, new sounds
To stay forever present.

Separation

Each presumes a longer knowing
Than the other;
Presumes the virtues of a greater
Understanding.
Lying in the empty dark,
Averted faces
Turning to some unknown grace,
Form clotted sounds of speech,
At any rate some small attempt
Towards communication.
Trying to untie the knot that somewhere formed
To strangle their two lives.
Trying in that large conjugal bed
To find the bliss they wrongly thought
Was theirs.
Strange soundless tears sweep down her cheeks;
His face stares, tortured, through the night.
Caught within their armour-suited selves,
Rusted, hardened through the years,
Each lies, incapable of real touch
However close they cling. Held within
The bondage of their own humanity,
They can but stare like ancient effigies
Into the black edged wings of night,
And mourn the tiny hours of their death.

Now

Promise me nothing;
Not the stillness of possession,
Nor a passion's unslaked thirst,
But rather let an ever present hour
Float soft as thistledown
Upon the secret dreaming of our thoughts,
That in such freedom
We should never lose
The innocence first born of joy,
Should never find frail strands of love
Fettered by a memory's sigh;
But rather that our eyes, awake, aware,
Should through ourselves, discovering,
Gaze through many different doors
Upon new worlds, while rainbow dreams
Arching down a rainy sky
May in their golden ending truly be
Proof of all that we may own
Within this timeless, living hour.

Reflection

How to explain the sudden cease of time?
A moment drifting through our busy lives
That somewhere stopped and scooped our fraility
Into eternal arms. The quiet reflections
Held in the silent pool, of trees and clouds
Lie captured, perfect; birdsong imminent
With endless soaring joy, caught on a coloured
Wing. The rustled touch of a lazy breeze
Within the leaves, and drift of butterflies
Across the hazy span of afternoon,
Suspends. like ripeness of a golden fruit,
Into eternity. The metronome
That pulse over pulse beats out the distant sound
Of life, like your body, sleeping soft
Beneath my hands, is lost to endless dreams;
And as I gaze, immensity of sky
In soaring blue, infinity of thought
Like cumulous amassing, the true fact
Of touch lies, as the stones beneath my knees,
Immediate in moment, here and now,
And all existence captured, perfect, still,
Is pure awareness to an endless moment
Bright as the shapes reflected in the pool.

To Talk of Love

To talk of love
Is to speak of transcience ~
A cloud-filled sky
That knows no rest,
Like the look of yesterday,
Is unable of itself
To prove its faith ~
Today, the passionate,
Lingering kiss
Can never be repeated
Quite the same tomorrow.
Deeper, calmer, frailer, dead,
Each moment is divided
Of itself and individual.
So, to reiterate
The word of love
Suggests inconstancy,
Or fear of loss,
Or the hopeful thought
That repetition soon
Will make it so
Like this or that;
Our strange and human souls
Still unaware
That love will rest
Most deeply where
Most quietly given,
And lingers longest
When most gently held.

A Gathering Tear

Do not think I grieve,
Or even that sorrow's
Played so large a part
Throughout my life;
Rather that true joy and sorrow
In the purity
Of height and depth
Seem so closely linked.
That searing, heaven-sent
Ecstasy of being
Pains quite as much
Through knowledge
Of its transciency
As its grey counterpart
Of grief ~
       And so I hang
A gathering tear
In the vast unblinking
Worldly eye;
Who knows, should I be happy
With a tiny drop
Of each emotion,
Thus hopefully feeling less,
Than with a chalice
Brimming from its depths
To fresh eternities?

The Hunter's Horn

Sitting here where summer sprawls and rolls
In green voluptousness before my eyes;
Caught in the deep content of man and soil,
Where suddenly vision is sharpened, limited
To fact; intricately simple,
Stem upon stem of varied flowers
And tousled grasses, rustling soft
Beside my novice ear. Now and only now
Can reality become a dream and the true dream
Of simple living change to reality.
Countless hours of indecisive living
Numbering less than a couple spent
In true awareness. Thoughts that mingle,
Share their birth. Looks not flirted,
Thrown away, but truly meant.
To every act a density,
Total involvement, measured for worth
By truth; sparked to life by love
Of being, joy of existence
Caught in the running wind across a field.
Now, and only now can the hunter's horn
Sound clear through the noisy living of my soul.

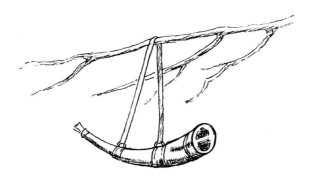

Martin in Concert

See through the man,
It is the voice evokes
Sere past
With honeysuckle hope,
And sounds the crystal horn
Down ageless years
Of woven song.
It is the voice awakes
Our dull, material minds
To reach again
For that free gaiety of life
That springs from minds
All wonder-new.
... The hall is filled,
Our lives are overflowed
With clash and din of sword and steel,
Triumphant laughter,
And soft, tender words
That yearned through other hearts,
Yet call us too
To wear upon our sleeve
The favour, sweetly made,
Of life and love.
... The last note sounds,
And dreaming eyes return
To focus on their own reality,
Yet still the thread that spins
Weaving past and future
Within this ever present hour
Will hang in memory.
The voice evokes,
The instrument still lives.

Glimpsed from the Car....

Premonition of my Mother's Death

On mellow autumn days like this one now,
Kind friends push out the chair,
That she may see the softly reddening bough
And feel the shimmering air;
Still hoping by such small acts to perform
A miracle of life,
And turn away the grey and gathering storm
The endless paining strife.
Moving behind the chair they cannot see,
(Or do they also fear?)
That though the face turns flower-like and free
Towards the warmth of air,
The sap is dying down,
Within the framework living now is done;
The head may nod, still listening through the pain,
Love and the body's worldliness may strain
To check for yet a while
What the eyes in their silent knowing
Darkly see across the mellowing day,
As kind friends push the chair upon the green
And daylight fades away.

Kontakion

For my mother

Yours is the rebirth
Swift to light and knowing,
For now you move as wind upon the ground
And spread your warmth like sun within our
    minds.
Now sorrow is fulfilled
And grieving done,
The stark tree of our lonely thought
Full blossoming.
For yours is the budding flower,
The scent of rose,
The dawn and evening colours down the lane,
As softly through the fleeting years
Your gift of love is spreading
In memories bright as butterflies
Upon a summer field.
For now your laughter's held upon the air,
Caught in the vibrant living of the house,
The sudden colour gracing eye and mind,
The endless presence running through our lives.
Now is the mystery infinite,
The circle closed;
Woman, lover, mother, wife,
You are returned
To that which is your knowing.
For yours is now the rebirth
Ours the living.

Reflection

The face from the other world
Has tears upon it,
Or so I would believe
Were I not from the outside
Looking in
Confused by the rain
That falls upon the pane.

The face from the other world
Has eyes that see
Spring dawn upon the hills
In varied greens,
And clouds that run before
A freshening breeze,
Or so I would believe,
Were I not from the outside
Looking in
Confused by reflections
Made of darker hues.

The face of this other world
Has lips that move,
Or so I would believe
Were I not
Confused by the tears, the rain,
The darkening hues;
Confused by the memory
Of having known this face,
And stronger fear
That I should be
From the inside looking out,
And not from the outside
Looking in.

Only When

Only when this vastness
Glimpsed without,
In spaciousness seeps through
My aching heart,
And rushes like a cleansing wind
Through this strange citadel of bones,
To spread its light, breadth, width,
Through veins and arteries
And through the vaulted body of my life;
Only then, when this deep vastness
Can be known within,
And hold a sovereignty of space
Kinglike and sure,
Can I, in humbleness,
Begin to know the glory,
And the quietude that springs
From this most holy breath,
Begin to know the point
At which 'I' cease
And consciousness begins.

Tree Dream

Growing from within, one day I saw
The tree in all its truth;
Mists had cleared to clean-lined clarity,
And brilliant colours flared
To show the naked thrust and singing strength
From earth to sky full growing.
First, the unpretentious, grassy bank,
Quiet peacefulness of earth,
Through which the mighty spreading roots were plunged
In knowing, first belonging.
Then the girth of trunk, four quarters fused,
And welded with a power
So sure that quivering branches skyward sprang
Their vaulting ecstacy,
As if to search and touch beyond all form
An endless universe.
The colours all were vivid, from the bark
Which blazed with an alchemy
Of green-gold life, to the stark and outlined
Tracery of branch upon a deep and trembling blue.
And so, with an inward, dreaming eye,
I saw most outwardly the tree's great truth,
And bowed my head in awe.

Picking Sweet Peas in the Rain

Arms stretched, but ever upwards,
To pick the final tendrilled flower,
I'm crucified, it seems, upon
A bank of glowing scent;
Caught in a moments dark desire
To capture that which now exists
Only in transcience.
And how my face in longing turns
To iron-grey skies for grace,
And how the answer finds release
In soft ablution on that place
Which is most dry and burnt.

Water streaming,
Water pouring,
Over scented petals soft;
Tears that from
My eyes are falling
Mingled with a certain grace;
Guilt of fear,
Of longing calling,
Washed away, streamed from my face;
Cleaner, brighter,
Gentler, lighter,
Calls a voice from that quite place.
New beginnings,
Never-endings
Moving in a radiant space.

Arms stretched but ever upwards,
To feel the gift of that soft shower,
I'm born again, baptismal rites
Of water, clean and pure,
Have stayed that moments dark desire,
And everything that now exists,
Exists so, free and sure.
For now my face in quietness turns
To clearing skies, for grace,
And now the answer rests and waits
As soft green shoots spring from that place
Which was most dry and burnt.

Visit to a Miraculous Shrine near Dachau

The Miraculous Shrine of Altötting
(Our Lady of) (not far from Dachau)

Love broods
With warm and glowing wing,
Above this place of peace;
Deep seated in the strength of time,
All hallowed by the candle flame
Of pilgrim prayer,
Life breathes its ease
Within a golden womb of light.
Here human fear dispels
Beneath the calm serenity
Of holy, ancient gaze;
The aching heart of hope
Knows peace at last,
As fed upon the food of faith
The wanderer kneels
Before the shimmering shrine.
Here it would seem
All things may live,
Because the soul of man
Knows perfect trust;
By man, with man, for man,
The tension grows
Achieving immortality
And status far beyond the human right;
How strange the power of this,
Which should flow large and limitless,
Is so confined to tiny statue, candle, church;
That man, in his darkness, crying out,
Cannot admit to such light everywhere.

Visit to Dachau

Hope dies;
The air seems hard to breathe,
And colour fades
Across the strangely waiting square,
For all is emptiness,
No hate, nor sorrow clings
With aching memory
To haunt the air;
But rather find
Man's inhumanity to man,
Rejection and denial
Of all that lies within him, proud,
Has made a truth of death
(If death is ceasing)
And left a place
Untouched by breath of life,
By it's own evil self destroyed
And sentenced to become
An empty sterile void ~
...   Now with a stark
Yet undemanding plea,
The black memorial stands;
The crown of thorns
Etched, groping on a cloudless sky,
Turns to become
Charred, twisted forms of men,
Emaciated, hurled through hell,
Their timeless, silent scream
But rarely heard
Beyond the walls where life is warm and gay.
Their endless plea for human right
Unheeded and as fragile as the thistledown
That drifts across the empty square.

Student WRAC's Lament

Dear General,
  We long
  To join in the throng
  Of the marching cadets
  On the Square.
  But the skirts round our knees
  Seem designed more to squeeze
  Than to lengthen our stride,
  Should we dare.
  But if we were pleated,
  Culotted, or treated
  To a few inches more
  Everywhere,
  Our step with the boys
  Would be worth all the noise
  And the Staff Sergeants
  Would not despair.

Kind General,
  We're proud
  That we've been allowed
  To train at this wonderful place,
  But to show we could drill
  With the neatest of skill,
  Would strengthen the feminine case.
  So give us a try,
  (Your fears we'll belie)
  As we stand on parade
  Oh, so surely;
  All shining and sweet
  From our hats to our feet
  And skirts flowing
  Oh, so demurely!

Cowslip

All summers born of childhood
Sang within that single flower:
How the thrush's egg glowed bright and warm
Within the confines of the hedge,
And wonder filled the tiny space of child
To see life so enclosed.
How mornings bore a magic alchemy
That spun so long into the swelling day
All time was lost in meadow warmth
And lazy drone of bee.
And how the trembling gold of this small flower
Was goal and prize to tiny hands,
As grasses whispered soft in listening ears
And cloudless skies reeled blue above.

Now from an autumn world of deep content
Those far-off days, kingfisher bright,
Still flash their magic through the dreaming mind,
As time condenses, child and sage are one
In wisdom springing from the self same well.

New Coinage

How impotent my mind to spill the words
From heart to pen;
To lay upon the waiting page
This ache of love.
How strangely poor a world that cannot mint
New coinage for an ever-changing state,
Debasing to a common term
Such natural, precious stock.
Imagination leaps, then falters back;
This joy, this pain,
Translated to a word,
No longer holds its unique awe,
Bonded to the living act of you and me.
And so it seems,
To hold integrity we must demand
A dumbness from our outer selves
That's perfectly transferred
Through symbols coined in look and touch,
And from such disciplines of trust
Mint wealth that is for us alone.

Lovers

Hermaphrodites are we,
That caught in love,
We rise, each from the other's loins,
So beautifully and free.
For each seeks endlessly
Their perfect, other half,
And the mind knows restlessly
Its finite part.
And so it seems that you and I
Remain no more,
But each as to the other grows:
The man by woman held,
And she by him deep-filled,
Till tossed within that thundering sea
The broken halves are joined,
The world is stopped,
And for a timeless beat
The seeking is no more.

On the Theme of Haiku

1

A petal falls
Upon the silent pool:
There is reflection.

Your love falls
Upon my silent heart:
Two halves are made a whole.

2

Here are all things met
Beneath this tree,
The spirit in the boughs,
The earth voice that is me.

Stonehenge

A litany of legend lost in a green field plain,
A requiem of stones sung for the source of light,
That lies forgotton now, it's vision blurred
To empty eyes, its secrets dissipated, gone,
Its mystic memory a wordless night.

For captive now within our harsh desire
To keep, to hold, these tragic prisoners stand
Immortal monuments, and through their silence speak
To listening ears, of times when man still moved
With earth and sky, still knew the elemental
Spirit of the soul, where birth and death
Were but the ritual cycle of the year
And holy in themselves, where the beat of life
Within the earth rang echoing through the heart,
And the deep held secret of the god of light
Shone bright in summer solstice skies.

To Peter with Love

Here where the steep slopes sing
Their strong descent to passive depth below,
In summer, softened, swayed with herb and
flower,
The hum of bee and endless quiet of days,
In winter purified with gift of snow
And starker spirit peace.
A simple name carved lonely on a stone
Stares blind to human eye
And changing years;
For few in passing by
Have hearts to know
That here the finite
Is the infinite,
Here more than memory lives
And sighs upon the wind~
Here was the spirit never born
Nor died; will never cease
Upon the flow of time,
But birthless, deathless,
Finds the inner gaze
Of perfect liberty,
At one with the earth and sky
And the steep slopes song.

Secret World

Still as a moments thought
The irises thrust purple heads
Against a cloudless sky;
The mayflies circle
And the gold fish bask
In liquid warmth beneath the sun;
Deep from their secret damp
The ferns unfurl
And the air hangs heavy,
Musked with scent.
Here all is secret
Springing from the earth
With timelessness of ancient way;
Here are my thoughts translated
To that point where no thought is,
And my body quite dissolved
To nothingness, yet
Beating with a heart that is all hearts
And laughing with a joy
That is all joys.
Now that I am no more
My true existence manifests
In flower and leaf and spinning star.
And what is yet to be is somehow past,
And what is past has yet to be,
For all is now, and moving with the world.

Nichola, Growing Up

Now from the pale seas
Of childhood dreams,
She rises, glimmering;
Soft-washed with secrets
And strange hidden thoughts,
Hers is the crescent moon
And the half-filled cup,
The trefoiled footsteps of awakening.
For now, as her green,
And sea-remembering eyes
Gaze wistfully back
To what was known and loved,
Life, like a curly-headed boy,
Laughs loud and beckoning.
And following those golden limbs,
She drifts across the shimmering sands
To where the world waits darkly strange,
And unknown shadows fall.
Now running through the clinging woods
New tears brim to her eyes,
Till suddenly, within a gated field,
All flower-filled and bright,
The unicorn is seen, his fabled horn
A sword of trembling light,
And as he lays his head upon her lap
The woman-child cries out in joy,
And the tapestry begins.

Sequestered Lord!

Sequestered Lord!
Between the trees, where moss springs secretly,
I lay my tears like diamonds at your feet;
Long the knowing, dark the sorrow,
Fern-furled, springing shy;
Deep-shafted, too, the joy that shines
Like sunlight through the leaves;
Deep-dreaming Lord!
Between these trees
There grows no time, no age,
Only the crystal flowing dream
That overfills the cup;
Here stands but the small divide of shape
Imprinting loneliness,
And the quiet depths of the waiting pool
As the waterfall sings through it.
This is the secret place,
Sequestered Lord!
This is the birth of all beginnings
And the knowing of all ends ~
These boulders here, this pool,
This waterfall,
This wood of trees and lives.

Ave Atque Vale!

Ave atque Vale!
In my beginning
So lies my end.
Through the darkness of my birth
Until the light that is my death
The windows open wide
On hidden lonely lands,
To where the rose tree
In the desert stands,
And the distant waterfall
Is mere illusion
Down a corridor of time.
To where the black ship sails
Across the dark horizon
And the old man's lonely leap
From crimsoned cliffs
To predatory sea
Is but a ripple
On the silent pool.
Ave atque Vale!
In my small beginning
The first stroke was drawn,
A sickle shining moon;
And in my end
The circle will be joined
Until there is no knowing
Which was birth
And which was death,
For all is endless
Held within
The curving roundness of the stroke.

Too Human Far ...

Gazing at the view
They thought they looked
Down at the winding river
And its plains.
Standing hand in hand
They still mistook
The haze of summer
And the swaying grain
As pure expression
Of a season's time,
And could not yet perceive
A passion's rhyme
In cloud and leaf.
Had they but known
They would have found
Colours of a deeper hue,
And birdsong imminent
Upon eternity;
They would have turned again
To where the hill
Rose in immensity,
And scaled it still.
But hand in hand,
Caught in the commonplace of life,
They took the road
That plainly showed its ease
Too human far,
Retracing their faint tracks
Through swaying trees,
They chose the path that led them back.

Because I Come...

Because I come, a dreamer, to this place,
Unknowing still of shape or form,
Yet strangely filled with all the tears of being;
Because I come, encumbered, bowed
With rich possessions gathered through the years
Of endless lives, am proud
With vain humility and hollow laugh;
And yet, because I come, am seeking, drawn
To this bright present shining like a jewel
Within a darkened cave, have gazed
Yet never seen; because of this
Will that deep voice sound in my thoughts
That teaches all things in entirety?
Will fear and emptiness all fade away
In one quiet outbreath of release?
Will he who sits and waits beside the cave
Unroll the stone and take me by the hand
To that bright citadel that shines within?
That I may see and know and find a form
That is all forms, yet changeless within time,
Because I come, a dreamer, to this place?

Transmission

Fusion of the senses, soul and mind,
With him who stole my living days
And turned my idleness
From empty love to overflowing joy,
Till I became the source of all that is.
An elemental vessel through which poured
All suns and rains,
All earths and raging winds;
And in becoming less, I then became
Much more than I had ever known.
 For now as peace enfolds my being
This small divide of shape
Forgets its separateness
And holds in memory,
Most pure, most sure,
Its endless joy.

Skol!

(Shakespeare style) [*]

O, what sweet death to drown within thine eyes!
To lift the crystal cup that holds my soul,
To dare the hidden light that all men prize,
And fathom mine own self to that loved whole.
How hesitant a step that first swift glance
Between the sparkling shallows of my mind
Is lifted up with glory at the chance
To pledge yet once again, and deeper find
My true intent in secret, hidden pools
Of thought requited, to feel the waters flow
And close above my head, let passion's rule
Grow quieter, and my beating heart rest so.
To find this death within thine eyes but proves
My glorious rebirth to the state of love.

Minterne Parva

These hills enfold me;
With a deep primeval strength
I'm gathered to their breast
And comforted;
Soft fields and country peace
Close round me, soothing, kind,
To lull my racing, city mind
With whispered song of flower
And leaf, until I merge,
A tiny part of this great world,
Lost in its calm consciousness
And insignificant.
For suddenly, the columbine
Trailing its lovely beauty
Through the hedge, has meaning more
Than all the busy acts of life,
Existing of itself
In true perfection to the scheme of things.
And as I lie, still cradled
By the earth, encircled by the dying sky
My heart is aching
With fullness of deep joy,
Sighing with the anchorite
Of long ago,
'Sin is behovely,
All shall be well,
And all manner of thing shall be well.'

Prayer

Now, when the air is bright
And the dance is swift.
When the body beats
To the pulse of earth
And the seed is honoured
As the flower loved.
Now, especially now,
Remind me, Lord,
Of that great space
That is your peacefulness.
That I being busy
In a busy world,
May not forget
From what still centre
I first sprang;
May still remember
That vast universe
Held deep within,
Filled with the rushing wind
Of holy breath,
Expanded into spaciousness
So deep, so wide,
The mere mind dizzies
And the body fades,
While self is but a tiny speck
Lost in the shimmering air.
Remind me, Lord, remind me, Lord!
That while the beauty of the world still calls,
Yours is the beauty I would know,
Yours is the peace where I would rest,
Unwanting.

Tribute to Jan de Hartog

Goodbyes are over,
But the Storyteller leaves his words
Like coloured birds
Darting through the shadowed leaves;
His thoughts still linger
On the lettered page
And, gifted to us, magical,
His essence still pervades.
Now myth and legend intertwine,
Leave golden threads in tapestries
Both rich and rare,
But the Storyteller weaves no more
For the rose once thrown for Icarus
Has withered in the evening sun,
And the haywains trundling through the dusk
Are harvest high.
A strange enigma of a man ~
Half bible, half salt sea ~
The Storyteller turns his eyes
Towards another land.
Passing the outer buoy of his own life
He rides on deep, uncharted seas,
His boat a single sickled sail
Against the darkening sky
And the world's far rim.
Now we are left; goodbyes are done.
We cannot weep, but must rejoice
For the Storyteller leaves his words,
Like coloured birds,
Like butterflies ~
Like love.

Jack and Nell

Oh, Jack he was a sailor,
And Nell she was a whore,
And both had known the wide, wide world
And seen it all before.

For Jack he liked the ladies,
And Nell she liked the men,
But neither felt the words of love
Though they spoke them now and then.

Now Jack returned from sailing
And rapped upon Nell's door.
"Come down! Come down! You lazy lass,
I've gold to show ~ and more!

Nell she like a guinea,
And a golden sovereign too;
She quickly clattered down the stairs
Her dress still all askew.

Side by side they mounted
Up to Nell's little room;
And laid upon the small hard bed
In the crimsoned, curtained gloom.

They thought not much about it
In the hot and fetid night,
But did what they had always done
By the guttering candlelight.

Then suddenly Jack trembled
As on Nell's face he gazed,
For his heart was filled with strange delight
And his eyes grew soft and dazed.
For Nell lay quite transfigured
In the softly glowing dawn,
And her heart was filled with tenderness
For the man held in her arms.

For love had entered quietly in
And bound them one as one,
And the memory never left them
Brief though it was, and done.

Song

Always apart,
Always.
The quivering heart
Burning alone,
Apart always.

Never together,
Never
In cool brown earth
To lie forever
Together.

Only after
The tears
And the death,
Comes laughter,
The rising together,
Forever, after.

Beyond the Outer Buoy

In tribute to Jan de Hartog's book 'The Outer Buoy'

Beyond the outer buoy,
Beyond the opposites of light and dark:
Pleroma and the void;
Beyond infinity, and far beyond that too,
The chartless wastes lie waiting.
The word made manifest draws only
In straight lines of knowing.
Pure thought expands, explodes,
And leaves a million stars
In dusty galaxies.
What must we do to name this nameless sea?
What things forget, what deaths relive
To glimpse the first eternal rim
Or ordered chaos?
Beyond the outer buoy of this white moon,
That sucks our oceans,
Sucks our bodies too,
With seasoned tidal pull, like answering like,
There waits our own forgetting;
And in the formless origin of all that is
Each knows his god in what he has believed
Once, long ago, upon the earth.
Beyond this outer buoy, beyond, beyond,
There lies an inner reach of harbouring
Where all things rest
Held in the swirling vortex
Of dark dynamic calm.
In this great nemesis,
Made one with all,
Homogenised towards a greater bliss,
Alone we drift,
Drawn to the greater mass that is our all,
Beyond, beyond, beyond the outer buoy.

(*The Outer Buoy is NASA'S name for the moon)

Astronaut

Earth-bearer, now I float above the moon's dark edge,
Umbilicus to lunar module taut and undelivered;
A stranger lost in space,
A foreign body, tissued soft,
Amongst the hurtling meteorites.
There is no other life, no other time
That was not now,
Only this thin suspension in the dark
And endless reach of all that seems
To hold my knowing.
The fourteen moons of Jupiter,
The rings of Saturn,
The goddess Ishtar named
Upon the heights of Venus;
The asteroid of Icarus
Proclaiming immortality gold winged:
The whole Olympian field.
Far, red-eyed Mars and Neptune too,
Are held, like me, in solitary suspension
Within the silent sigh of space.
What more is there to want
What more forget?
Why ever think again of that swift pace
That we call life?
All lies here, all lies
Hanging within this moment now,
As I am drowned in captive ecstasy
Before this dream of spinning space.

I glance around, and there,
Radiant with colour as no other,
Swirling with varying blues of sea,
Distant with green and gold of land,
Misted with nimbus of high-streaming cloud,
There rises, quarter size,
The earth's bright rim.
Now, suddenly, all memory swells
With urgent recollection of deep love:
The place where I belong,
Where first was spawned the single cell
That grew and multiplied until this moment now,
Until this very moment when I stand,
Earth-bearer, caught upon the moon's dark edge,
Unfettered in a void of space,
Alone, unlike all others that have yet been known ...
A voice speaks flatly from the radio,
I am recalled
The dream is gone:
I float, an ordinary man, in outer space.

Past Life?

I am passionate with love;
Molten with your deep desire.
Refined to bladed sharp delight.
Dark Singer, only let your words
In secret sequence loose my joys
Through hidden honied caves.
Seed me, Singer of dark songs,
Seed my mouth, my ears, my mind,
With words that riot, call, inflame.
Mark the tight-furled graven scroll
With wanton song.
Shock the marble, unlined brow
With wilful, wild semantic play.
Let the monkey in his fez
Leap with bright and jabbering joy;
Let the dog wait for his feast.
Sing, sing, dark Singer,
Strike thy lyre,
Tear wide my boredom with your songs
And seed my very soul, that I may feel
No quivering of the lyre but by your touch.
Awaken me with fingers drawn
Across orgasmic deep delight.
Words, words and only words
Across the music of the lyre
That bends and twists the ecstasy
Plucked from its swelling soul.

Let young men pour their seed across my
      breasts,
Their quivering sharp and swift,
Their heads cast down.
FOR I AM BORED.
Oh, Singer of the endless song, I need thy words
To seed my fecund mind; I need thy wantoness,
Thy laughter flaunted in the face of Rome.
Tame me with your wild seed,
Awake our bodies, flame our minds
To that delight that opens hidden doors through
      words;
Let our laughter ring both sides of paradise,
For we are gifted with the gods own joy
Of recognition: to us our love was glorious then,
Is now, and still to be; the silver seeding
Timless on the yet unfinished scroll.

First of the Apostles

How could she know, how could she even see,
Tears double-visioning, blinding all before her?
Only the sudden recognition of the voice,
The nuance of her spoken name
And the bliss that filled her being ~
Filled the very source of her life's flow ~
As suddenly she realised all was well.
He lived! The pain within her
Dissipated in the dawn;
The air was numinous, trembling at the edge
Of his known presence,
And joy returned.
'Rabboni? The word was hardly breathed ~
A distillation on the air ~
But still she hesitated, still ~ then dared,
'Rabboni!' once again, the fullness of her heart
Compelling her to reach, to touch
And to confirm his living form.
But no. The hand was raised,
A barrier to human love,
Rejecting all she longed to say.
The gates of heaven closed once again,
A second time her eyes sprang tears.
Not touch him? The words were hammering like nails
Into the coffin of her soul.
She who had held his feet upon her lap
And washed them with her very tears,
Who loved him most in all the world.
Not touch him?

Then she heard the voice again,
Like sunshine over darkened hills,
'Come, my Mary. come now, come
And dry those tears.
Rejoice with me for sin is now atoned
And death destroyed.
Go, Mary, go and tell it all.
This is the utmost moment of your life;
You are the first, for you within your love
Have seen and recognised and known.
Go, go and spread your news.'
And so she ran,
Barely looking back to where he stood,
Light framed in dark,
As all the joy of heaven beat in her ears
Cascading through the wakening day
Like blossoming trees.
He was alive!
And she was the first ~ the messenger!

Centurion's Lament

Gone is the sword from my side, the sword that is Rome,
And the scabbard that slapped on my thigh,
Like the wave on a painted ship,
Grows silent, lost into time.
Gone is the sword from my side, the sword that is Rome;
As the eagle bright with the hopes of men
Dulls in the wind and the rain, so the body's toil
Weakens the heart that longs for home.
Gone is the sword from my side, the sword that is Rome,
And gone is the virtue, gone from the years of peace;
Now rent is the purple robe; yet the passing of time
Can never erase the life once lived,
Dim though the dream of it seems,
As gone is the sword from my side, the sword that was
Rome.

Dream

I lay within your arms and I was dead;
Cold water dripped from hair and clinging clothes,
Limp body falling from your fierce embrace
Could not revive the fire of living warmth,
For life was snapping on a golden thread.

I lay within your arms and I was dead;
But, oh, your kisses I could feel and know.
And how I longed to comfort and to hold,
To chase away the pain from your sad eyes,
But I was spinning on a golden thread.

I lay within your arms and I was dead;
But I was calling down a spiralled void,
That you should hear, hear once again
My words of love that echoed longingly,
Though I was drowned and in your arms and dead.

I lay within your arms and I was dead;
If I could feel your kisses, could you hear
My words of love? Oh, could you somehow know
That all was well, that I would always wait
Till life had snapped again its golden thread?

Wearyall Dream

Here, where the thorn tree blooms
In sere December, blossoming white;
Where the staff of Joseph
Carried from a distant land
First seeded knowledge of the Cross.
Here, in Avalon, where legend leapt
From greening lands of opalescent mist,
As the Fisher-King lay dying, maimed,
For want of the question that was not asked,
And the Grail out-poured its blood-red wine
Across a wasteland sorrowing.
Here, on Wearyall Hill,
Where the hawthorn stands and the Tor,
A thrusting mystery of power, is seen;
Here, in my humanity, I dream
That once again the nail-pierced feet
Heal the path of suffering,
And, newly heard, the words resound
"Come unto me all you that labour
And I will give you rest
This day, and always, will you be
With me in Paradise."
Shall we now also rise
And in the morning of our souls
Drink of this overflowing cup?
Is paradise the eternal now
Of union with the Christ within
If only we believe it so?

Here, where the thorn tree blooms,
Hope-ribboned on the hill,
I wake and wonder: was it just the wind
That blew those words,
Well-known yet somehow never heard?
Or did the Spirit bend and speak
Above the grasses whispering heads,
Filling that place of silence deep within?
What sudden comprehension tore the veil
That all the wonder of His risen light
Should thus be seen
Across the trees, across the hills
Showing that paradise indeed
Not only rests in heaven
But here on earth within ourselves.

Visitation

Somehow, within that souless hotel room,
Filled with the dying day and a city's sighs,
They fell in love; somewhere they found
An alchemy which ground the dross of lust
To shining gold.
Unnoticing at first,
Caught in the vortexed passion of a kiss,
They did not feel the change, nor see
The sudden light,
The tall winged angel entering,
The scattering of dust.
Only when they sighed
And opened wide their eyes,
Did each, within the other, find
Something more than they had seen before
Only then did breath suspend
And words fall silent,
Only then did each heart
Beat quite differently
And something of eternity was born.

Iona

Island of sudden change,
Of paradox;
Where the dove-man walks
Bone-whitened shores,
And the heavens echo deep
In pebbled pools.

Island of rushing winds,
Where the voice of God
Sweeps tussocked hills,
And the hermit's cell
Is a litany of wordless joy
Caught between sea and sky.

Island of ancient lore,
Of legend, myth,
And sacred space
Circled by foaming seas;
Where prayer has seeped for centuries
Through rock and stone.

Island that opens wide
The veiled eye
To deeper seeing,
Dissolving boundaries
Like a single wave
That slowly breaks across eternity.

No ache of sorrow here,
No memories pain.
Time ceases: all is still
As the wings of the Paraclete
In brooding holy wisdom beat
Above this sacred isle,
And we are whole

Peace

Slow down, my heart, and know the ease of now;
There is no hurry in this present hour,
No rush, no speed,
Only the quiet unfolding of the bud,
The dewdrop trembling on the leaf
The distant hum of bee.

How good, my heart, this cup of flowing life,
This open moment's full discoveries,
No tears, no fear,
No future hopes, no pain of past regrets,
Only the sighing of the breath
Gifted with pure release.

Consider now, my heart, this act of love,
This giving to the gods of all that comes,
In trust, in joy;
This practice for eternity that falls
With radiant ease about the day ~
This ever-living hour.

In Memoriam

(September 11th, 2001)

Agnus Dei!
Innocent he runs
Across a field of sorrow;
Guiltless, fearless,
knowing only love,
He bears with
firm intent, in
child's hands,
a trinity of crosses.
He cannot know, but we in our guilt have learnt
How the past must crucify, while the present
Here and now is made impure and daily slandered
Through man's fear and greed. and the third, what
Of the third, the unnamed cross? Is that his future life ~
He who is every child? ~ Is that his earth reward for life
Begun in loving innocence?
What will he grow towards,
this light-filled child,
A world of peace and hope,
Or long remembered
anger and revenge
Engraved upon his heart?
And later, when he hangs in
solitary crucifixion,
Unclear as to why he dies,
Will the words 'I love you'
fall redeeming,
Cleansing from his lips?
Echoing down the
shifting shores of life
In glorious recollection
Of all that truly is,
and was and will be,
Before the purification
Of the blast, the flames,
the sudden death.
Agnus Dei!

103

Walking through the Woods in Baarn, Holland

I'll fill my heart with trees:
Tall conifers that pierce a deepening sky,
Resinous upon the summer air;
The girth of oak,
The grace of beech,
The sapling strength of alder.
Down avenues of gothic branch
And quivering leaf,
I'll find a vaulted place of prayer;
From firmest root to tallest bough,
Green and vibrant, rising strong,
I'll let this essence sprung from mystery
Of primal earth and sighing air,
Strengthen and heal;
I'll find it numinous within myself,
A blessing as I pass, a wanderer
Enriched with holy, greening life.

The Veil Rent

Bored; immured
In the darkness made of doubt;
My heart's well springing blood
Of pain and loss,
I wonder how it is that life without
Can move so freely, joyously,
Like high cloud on a distant sky.
I wonder how, as twilight glooms
The hidden valley, bird song should rise
In poignant, pure and liquid notes
Of clarity that feed a yearning
In my soul so complex, so refined,
So sharply made, exquisite in the subtle
Shades of want, that I am caught
Confused, as all reality
Becomes a shadow falling dark
Across a green-grassed hill.
The loss is loss of all, yet the pain
Becomes a dream,
And the dream a deep unbreaking wave
Within an ocean's swell;
For the notes once heard,
Fulfill a beckoning in the memory
That breathes simplicity,
And fills the fragile flowing cup of life
With crystal sound and light,
Splitting darkness,
And opening wide the present day
To all its living, glorious sacrifice.

Europa

Taurean arms; high-horned embrace,

That tosses dreams like galaxies

Across a midnight sky. The eye,

The bright, illumined eye,

Envisioned with the perfect mate

In grazing, green Elysian fields

Of cloven love..

How deep the union! arched across

An ocean's sighs. How full the roar

Through silent quivering ether sounds.

Europa's plunge to paradise

Is lost, in quivering passion lost,

In frenzied beauty drowned and lost;

Held by the bull-god, held and whored,

Loved beyond reason's measured gate,

And born within the horned embrace

To fabled immortality.

Leda

White through the gleaming rushes curved,
Entwined with thigh from dark depths glistening;
The outstretched wing, the searching beak,
The woman's pale ecstatic face.
The strangeness of the visitation stills
Dark wood and lake; the waters, mirror-like
And calm, reflect an evening sky.
All is quiet, no movement
But the Olympian swan,
In twining, silent coupling
Embraced and held.
No birds, no rustling of the leaves,
No breeze, only a trembling moment
As the world is stayed by silence, listening,
Waiting for the fusion, plunging dark
To secret depths until the fire is touched,
Until the heavens are opened wide
With dazzling light, and Leda's sky-borne cry
Thrills through the echoing woods,
Her body filled with the immortal flame
Lost now to human love for evermore.

Forgotten Love

Why were we wordless, speechless,
When the inner voice was clamouring so?
Why did we act as if we'd never touched
The silver chalice of the other's soul,
Nor briefly sipped the crimson liquid
Hidden there?
Why, when we walked through fields
Embroidered thick with meadow flowers,
Down lanes enclosed by wild rose,
When the sky was a shimmering
Gleaming blue, did we never turn,
Unlock the gates of our private selves,
And find the freedom that was ours
From the very first?

And then, when evening fell,
When the hill loomed dark against the starlit sky,
And Venus rose behind, I knew you had forgotten
What, once, love meant.

Separation

Separation is the lack of you;
And the lack of you a void,
Devoid,
Of life.
Separation is a dream of you,
That tantalises with reality
To twist the nothing round the with
And make a madman
Of normality.
Separation is the thought of you
That severs separateness
With constancy
Creating paradox within the words:
A longing now replete,
A dream the evidence
The fullness that is void.

Home

The benediction loops and far above
The grey sky shatters with a gleam of sun;
And swiftly slicing through the sharpened quiet,
A child's laugh stresses with a joyful line
The living moment hanging like a star.

Now down calm wings of night the trees
Ripple their strange tracery, with suppliant arms
Vaulting to the sky an endless prayer,
Till peace sighs down, folds and enfolds
The running minutes, and love and birth and death
Are frozen in one long eternity,
Timeless, as the benediction falls.

Thoughts while Picking Wild Cyclamen for Sue on Samos island

Do not ask why the world is cruel;
Why love is stoned
Beneath the rolling blue black clouds.
Do not weep for the joy now gone,
For the laughter flown
Across the span of passing years,
But rather walk where nature
Smiles and heals.
Where all exists within
The pattern of the now.
Grow like the flower, frail,
Perfect within the order of the day.
Smile in the rain, and spread
Your perfume. Sway
To the quick delight of windy days,
And when the sunshine comes
Then turn your head
Growing in the benediction
Of its warmth. Own
That all things rise and fall
Just as they should,
And when the dark clouds gather
Remember how blue the sky beyond,
And know that you are blessed
With all that God can give.

Holiday Postcard

He said he loved me, Mum;
He said he loved my breasts so small and bare.
He kissed me, Mum: not like the boys at home
All fumblings on the darkened porch,
But like he thirsted for me,
Thirsted for me deep and long
And could not get his fill.
And then ~ I know you told me not ~
He loved me then the dark night long
Till my whole body filled with song
And joy was bubbling in me like a spring
And I was overflowing on and on ~
I knew I would be his for evermore ...
.But when I woke, all tousled, tangled in the sheets,
The sun was shining hot into the room
And he was gone. Oh, God,
I've searched for him the whole day long.
His name was Tom, that's all I know,
And now he's gone. I think my heart will break,
That I might die,
Oh, Mum, oh Mum, I wish that you was here.

Five Holiday Postcards

Costavecchia

Secret, between olive groves
And clustered cypress;
Past fields splashed with red and blue,
And waving oats white-bleached with sun,
The dirt track winds. Ahead a hoopoe flies,
A pheasant calls and fireflies glimmer
In the dark of trees.
Enchantment fills the evening air
As wrought iron gates rise tall and straight
And, ivy-clad, the house appears
As if by sudden magic
Swift released from dreams.
Now is the beginning,
Now the time
When life's reality recedes,
An ebbing tide lost in the whispering wind;
And so the gentle easing of the mind
Begins with elemental song
Of sun and breeze,
Soft dappled shades, blue skies,
And laughter
Found with friends at ease.

Simi

Island of boat builders known since ancient times,
Where houses, softly pastel in the morning light,
Cascade through green of cypress
Into the turquoise sea below.
This bustling port entices,
Bright with spices, silver, fruits,
And streets that wind forever upwards ~
Eight glass hearts swing in a window frame
Sounding the breeze's passion as we pass ~
As up we toil, our morning walk
Past gardens tended during peaceful days,
And 'Calemera' whispers step on step
From timeless faces etched by life.
At last we crest the hilly reach,
Looking down upon the town,
Across the limpid sea to isles beyond,
Till, finally, the whitewashed church,
Our aim and end,
Crests like a wave
Above the tide of man's fast-moving life.

(Calemera means 'Good-morning' in Greek)

Nisseros

Strangest among these isles
With fertile slopes of almond, olive, fig,
Nisseros lies, Janus-like,
One verdant face turned soft towards the sea,
The other, formed of molten fire,
Sulphur-smoking, arid, harsh.
Within the town the narrow streets
Are overhung with balconies,
Flowers and bougainvillea
Bright against the white-washed walls.
The shaded square where people meet
To quietly pass the time of day,
Is dark with a canopy of trees
That's filled with busy chattering birds.
The ancient castle still maintains
Cyclopean walls, and the monastery still keeps
The peace of prayer,
While the Virgin of the caves,
With deep-souled eyes, looks out across the sea
To bless the brightly coloured boats
Of fishermen, to guard the sailor's homing.

San Antimo

Peace in a sun-filled valley;
A gentle breeze and cypress rising tall
Beside this solid edifice of man.
Within, the light-filled space
Is calm and cool. A holiness
Of centuries seeps through soaring arch
And pale translucent stone.
The purity of plain chant resonates
As healing balm,
While billowing clouds of incense
Blur the vision, wreathe and twist
Like wisps of long-forgotten memories.
Suddenly, beyond the clear
And columned pane,
High against the azure sky,
A dove is seen ~
The Paraclete himself ~
Descends with visioned wing.
Now earth and man and sky
All meet in loving sympathy
And all is well within this human space of time.

Tilos

Island of gentle bays
And seas so clear
The sun lays cobbles on its sandy bed.
Plunging cliffs
Of gold and brown
Cut into waters cobalt blue,
And the Sunday sound of bells
Calls from a white-washed chapel
Reached by stony paths.
Here the Angel Raphael stands guard
As we, in our small humanity,
Light waxen tapers
Within the cool and shadowed vault,
Say silent prayers,
And leave, enriched
By faith's simplicity.

Saint Francis Receives his Stigmata on Mount Alverna

(taken from my play Brother Sun, Sister Moon*)*

High on Mount Alverna,
Secret with hermits' caves
And the sudden rush
Of wind through storm-struck trees;
High on Mount Alverna
Where the eagle soars
And the sky loops down
With misty arms
To wreathe round craggy steeps;
Here, in nature's loneliness
The Saint would go to find his God
In prayer and solitude.

What can we know, or even understand
Of his deep longing?
How can our frail, and tempted minds
Begin to comprehend
Such saintliness,
Or ever find a like resolve
To suffer so willingly:
Near naked body, torn and bleeding feet,
Stomach taut with emptiness,
And yet ~ *somehow* ~ on fire within?

And at what moment ~ can we ever know?

Did soul transcend the flesh
And cause the heavens to open
As the vast winged seraph ~
Like a cross spread out
And filling all the sky
With crucified and flaming pain ~
Pierced the waiting soul
With his sword of pitying grief?

What silent ecstasy!
What transformation then
As mortal man
Was touched by the divine;
And when the heavens
Had closed again
Did the great mountain wait
Quite silent, still,
Until the Saint had opened wide his eyes
And, staring downwards,
Seen the marks of nails in his own hands?

Jessie Gell

Returning

It seems complete: returning, as it were,
To this far place that I have never known.
The hills of Quetta, stark and bare,
Are backdrop to a shimmering sky,
Echoing back a timeless peace
Across the sun-baked cemetery.
I am returning to the grandmother
Whose face I've never seen
(Except in staid Edwardian pose
Upon a faded page).

Her grave stands witness now
To her bright youth
And all the other brief, swift lives
Who died so far from home.
I stand before the marble cross,
Still straight, intact,
In spite of earthquake, dust and storm;
The letters,after ninety years,
Still black and clear.
I look at my left hand
And when I see the ring that once she wore ~
A ring of smouldering sapphires
Deeply blue as midnight sky ~
I feel a strong connection,
Born of blood, of love,
A sudden sadness that I never knew
The sparkle echoed in my father's eye.
Tenderly, I place some flowers,
Vibrant, bright upon her grave;
The chowkidar, close by,
Salutes with military respect,
As I, within my salutation, sigh goodbye,
For I may never visit here again.
... Across the dry, clear air
The muezzin calls the faithful
To their prayer.
A wind blows up, the hills of Quetta
Dim behind a dusty pall.
I glance back, once, and see the flowers
Blaze out across the arid waste.
It is as if, for one brief moment,
She had returned,
A spark of dancing life,
Acknowledging that I had come,
That she was not forgotten, ever,
Nor alone.

Ali Ishmael Abbas

(Daily Telegraph ~ April 2003)

At first you think he's crucified,
But, no, that's wrong;
He cannot hang suspended from a cross:
He has no arms,
Only a flame-seared torso
And the thin brown legs beneath.
He says he longs to die
Unless they find
Another pair of hands for him to use.
He says he longs to die:
He's twelve years old.

There is no case for war or peace,
No right or wrong, no good or bad;
We, each in our separate way,
Stand guilty, crying 'Crucify!'
Before this boy, this modern Christ
Displayed in suffering.
Is he the lamb brought to appease
That dark devouring god within us all?
For, should we wish to lay the blame,
We find no Judas in our midst,
No silver traded for the kiss of love;
Only our own betrayal as we forget
His pain when war is done;
When interest moves to other things
And leaves us standing
Damned in our faithlessness.

Progress of Life?

The sparkle,
The laughter,
The charm
And the fun.

> The soldier,
> The lover,
> The father,
> The friend.

The leader,
The courage,
The honour,
The fame.

> The garden,
> The flowers,
> The slippers,
> The home

... Now he's just an old man on a trolley.

Dementia

I cannot mourn: you left so long ago.
Left when the widening fissures of the mind
Swept clean our memories and like a child
You laughed, unknowing, for the day alone.
I cannot mourn, because we grieve,
Together, in the space where you are not,
And love, though cornered, still must breathe
In frail forgotten wisps of touch.
The shadowed shuffling slippered feet
Measure out a prison cell
Of mindless wandering,
Both yours and mine.
And anger, once unknown,
Racks the daily tasks with guilt.
I cannot mourn: there is no grief
And no escape,
Only the wide grey beach and the sucking tide
Of living death.

You Asked for a Poem

You asked me to enclose with words
That which is infinite.
You asked for a poem
That might describe
The beauty of these hills,
These vales,
As seen through the eyes of love.

I cannot.

No man can hold the light
Nor change the shifting shades,
The wreathing mists
Upon the mountain tops.
No man can grasp and bind
An essence,
The intangible residue of love
That our two hearts
With sighs and kisses
Have woven through the woods,
The streams, the hills,
The very sky.

Only the rainbow arching suddenly
Across a shower-filled plain
Can start to speak of that vast vision
That manifests such beauty in this world.

The Greater Part

Play me as you would a violin,
Drawing the bow across the waiting strings,
Invoking in the quivering swift response,
The heart of joy,
The truth of tears,
The flight of ecstasy.

Your movement first, your sound
Translated then by echoing back,
And yet ... not quite the same,
Not quite exact in every note,
But rather that the union of the two
In overtone and harmony, now finds
A greater part ~ a third ~
Whose music, sweeter still,
Finds height and depth
And passion more inspired
Than from that first beginning
When the one picked up his bow
And drew it, soft, across the sleeping strings.

Song

Down on the sands;
The beat of the sea,
The roar of the surf,
The ebb of the tide,
The fall of my feet
Down on the sand.

The thrift on the cliff,
The call of the gull,
The mussel-clad rock,
The slant of the sun;
The turn of my heart
With you by my side.

What can I know
Of the future to come
Like an incoming tide
Across soft, rippled sands?
Just the beat of my heart
With you by my side ~
What more can I know?

Song

Weave me a coffin twined with willow branch,
Where that which is the lesser part of me
May lie, unknowing, in the cool brown earth.
There let me rest as nature shifts and breaks
Impacted soil, until the singing shoots
Of greening life spear sightlessly
Towards the light. The willow knows no rest
But must, within that dark decaying damp
Revive, restore and resurrect,
Till that small grassy and forgotten mound
Becomes a sighing, swaying bower,
A living monument
Where once lay only death
And dark forgetting.

Songs for the Soul

They hang disguised as dreams
Or blossoms on a tree.
They wind around the poet's heart
Or slide an easy way
Down rainbow curves.
Glistening, shining in a tear,
Sighing on a lover's kiss,
Or breathing from a smile,
Within this brief eternal now
They leap, unsummoned, into life.
What is this stardust shimmering down
But all the soul's remembered joys
Tumbling from a waking heart:
The eagle's flight on golden wings
The dream of oceanic bliss,
The heavenly ecstasy.
Don't capture them,
But let them come,
Before the gateway of the mind
With laughter and with love.
Then set them free:
They are not yours.
They are a gift.

Inner Child

Abandoned:
In the womb,
The cot,
The tomb.
Forgotten, crying,
Turning loss to rage;
Bound by the hurt,
The bars, the cage.
Searching, seeking
One or other,
Absent father,
Failed mother.
Only the centre,
Circled, strong,
Can hold
The laughing child of song.

At the 11ᵗʰ Hour of the 11ᵗʰ Day of the 11ᵗʰ Month ~ A Village Remembrance

No stone memorial,
No names, black, sorrow-carved,
No bugle blowing through the silent day;
Only the tree cut down to make a cross
And the single flag in honour dipped.
Only the wind, haunted with ghosts,
Icy with chilling breath,
Only the crowd, wordless, grouping round.

Now, as the country stills in old rememberance
Of all it means to die for kith and kin ~
How courage takes its toll,
How minds and limbs are maimed
And spirits tortured with a living pain ~
It matters not the where or when,
The cenotaph or simple knotted cross,
Only that all should not have been in vain;
Only that present suffering,
Commingled with the past,
Should fade in tolerance;
That love should not lie bloody, strewn
Across the battlefields,
Nor terror echo in a child's eyes;
Only that all should not have been ...

Only that all should not have been in vain.

The Boy Theodore

(A song cycle never completed)

Child, sprung from the greening hills
That plunge towards surging seas;
Born from a wind that's laughter brimmed,
Curly haired and swift of limb,
You dance beneath dappled shade of trees.
Here is your life as clear, as clean
As silvered rills and flowing streams
Sliding through fern and mossy green.
Child, sprung from the greening hills,
Curly haired and swift of limb,
I hear your laughter echoing long,
Held on the salt sea breeze.

Boy, whose life is the greening hills,
Whose heart is tuned to nature's ease,
Never forget the fields that sing
Of the place that is home, of the love that clings
Like thrift to the windswept lea.
This is the soul of your inward dream,
A thread through the tapestry drawn unseen,
Through dark your light's unwavering beam.
Boy, whose heart is the greening hills,
I'll never forget the fields that sing,
Nor your love and laughter caught and held
Like a prayer on the salt sea breeze.

Thames View

Magical ~ just sitting here
With the brown silk river
Slipping slowly by
And the grey-green shore
Shingled, wet, extending into view.
Beneath my window;
Through the willow's laden fronds,
Water fowl contentedly
Patter over mirroring sands,
Pecking, dibbling at the weed
Cast by an ebbing tide.
A barge chugs past, canoes glide by,
Mere lines upon the waters face,
Their oars like glinting blades
Cutting the river's rhythmic flow.
 The gift is peace,
The soft enfolding peace
That calms the busyness of life,
And stillness, born of solitude,
That lets the sleeping spirit wake
And, like a coloured kite unloosed,
Fly free across the rivers flow.
Into the morning sky.

Lucifer

I saw him in his glory. Falling,
Tumbling through the darkened void,
Losing all he loved the most ~
The sight of God, the space of heaven.
He fell, a golden tangled mass
Of legs and arms, of hair and wings
And blazing, pain-struck eyes,
The farewell streaming from his mouth
A foaming galaxy.
On, on he fell,
A giant, prophetic comet
Streaked across the starry skies,
Still hurtling earthwards.
No other angel dared his grief,
His sacrifice,
As reaching earth's bright rim,,
His fiery splendour
Wavered, dimmed and died.
Now, dark lord of this our world,
Carrying the density
From which there is no birth;
Duality, new-coined, a choice
Where once there had been none,
He strides an outcast path,
A deep eternal longing
Heavy-chained around his heart.
For he alone, whose name is light,
Has dared to lose himself,
So to become
The very dark through which the Light
Might manifest.
O glorious Lucifer!

Emma

Where are you now?
Where are your thoughts
As your body lies, a mere disturbance
In the large conjugal bed?
Outside, unknowing, in the summer sun,
Our children play, their laughter
Spilling over the window sills
Filling the silent room
With joyous life.
Holding your hand I sit and watch
As your body's pain, clasped like a doll,
Tight within fragile arms,
Ticks away the morphine of your dreams,
Perhaps your very life,
Each sound a dagger in my heart ...
        ... The hours pass, a breeze
Lifts the drawn curtains; suddenly
Sunshine floods into the room, across the bed,
Across your face, so pale, so young.
And I think of how you sketched our sons
Once, as they lay sleeping, innocent.
But yours, I know, is the sleep of death,
For death is waiting, a grey but gentle form,
A quiet release, mere thistledown
Drifting across the fading afternoon.
No more than that, I know,
And you will not be gone.
And yet, and yet, I shall be left alone
And wondering ~ where are you now?
Oh, Emma, where?

Mystery of Mysteries

Mystery of mysteries!
Mysterious beyond all knowing;
Drawing from the waiting dark
What was, what is and always will be.
Mystery of mysteries,
Mysterious beyond all knowing!
Manifesting into light
The paraclete of Love's desire
To fire the formless into life
And temper through to alchemy.
From breath without to breath within,
This silent ecstasy sighs through
Each petalled flower and trefoiled leaf,
Each field and hill and blazoned sky,
Each stirring of the darkened world,
Whispering to our sleeping souls
Such glories that might make us wake,
Might make us long to see and know
That mystery of mysteries,
Mysterious beyond all knowing!

Lost Twin

Oh, you whom I love most!
Who moved with me within the womb,
Who blended, merged and swirled
In heavenly dance,
In endless unity.
That circled time
Of past eternity,
The colours changing,
Like the dawn, the sea ~
That vast and universal sea ~
Remain with me.
Oh, you whom I love most,
Why did you go?
Who called
That you could leave
Our soft simplicity,
Our timeless kiss,
Our symbiotic unity?
Why do you tantalise
With soft remembered smiles,
And memories
Like shooting stars
Lighting the darkened corners
Of my life.
Oh, you whom I love most,
Why did you go?

Pictures at an Exhibition

(on a theme of Mussorsky)

Like any other couple in the darkened gloom,
Studiously, with knowing air,
Moving from frame to frame,
Asorbing beauty through the painter's eye
Vicariously.
Like any other couple, it would seem,
Except that she,
In her wide-eyed wandering,
Sees only him, and he,
Through his nonchalant stroll,
Feels only her
Beating like his life blood through his veins.
She stops and gazes at a pastel nude,
All glistening thighs and breasts,
And knows the body somehow to be hers
Of just an hour ago,
Wiped over with a gleam of sweat
And soft with love. She sighs:
The honied glow of her content
Colouring all the scenes.
While he, musing before some beauty
Captured with downward look and flowing hair,
Finds recognition in the fact
That his own love, caught on the canvas
Of his memory, is lovelier still.
And so they wander, silently, from room to room,
Feeling only the others lust, their swift desire
Varnished across the paintings in the room;
Fooling the passing world with their intent,
Their private passion echoing back
Those human hopes and loves and dreams
Painted for public exhibition.

Off Course

'It's like a dream,' she said.
He said, 'The wind is dying down.'
'Sailing,' she said, 'on a silken sea,
Opalescent, calm.'
He said, 'The sails need letting out
A reef or two'.
'A dream,' she said.
'And check our chart,' he said,
'It could be shallow here.'
'Flying fish,' she whispered,
He replied, 'Not in these seas ~
Far too cold.'
'Or angels wings across the sky?'
He didn't hear.
'This breeze is like a kiss,
A secret that is ours.'
He said, 'I need to concentrate,
To see what problems lie ahead.'
She said, 'The only problem I can see
Is the distant gathering of clouds.'
But he, binoculars to eyes,
Was blind.
And so she wept ~
Unseen salt tears ~
And the lighthouse tolled
Its distant warning bell.

Geese Flying Overhead at the East Coker Poetry Evening

Poetry? they said, arching overhead
Great wings of sound;
Disdaining with long suppled neck
Our gathering below.
Our struggling verse,
Our metre, scansion, rhyme
And verbal traps
As, humanly, we try to hold
What they in all their natural ease
Display.
Now dark against the pale translucent night,
Skeined like victory,
With wild and lonely cry
Calling, calling to our hearts,
They pass, and so become,
Within their very act
Of wide-winged flight,
A living poem
Stretched across the sky.

His Death by Hanging

It was a violation:
His death, by hanging,
Early in the dawn.
It ricocheted through curtained living rooms,
Headlining TV news,
The tabloid press.
My body felt it,
Jolted, shocked,
Rooted for the moment to the spot
Where first the words impacted
Blow by blow
In raw, imposed collective guilt.
For evil walked to death
Contemptuous, calm and unafraid,
In spite of actions damned,
And darkness crushed,
In spite of living ended, done.
Hydra-headed still,
The dark untouched by light,
But now repaid in kind,
Will find a way
To resurrect, to rule again.
Soon, all too soon,
The twisted, rope-strung neck
Will spring a head that claims the martyr's
crown,
As we, the ignorant,
Whiter than white,
Claiming immunity from Moses' laws
Fail yet again to learn,
Fail yet again to even understand.

Ali Ishmael Abbas

(on television, four years on)

Not the boy's face now ~
The thin boy's face ~
But adolescent, handsome, softly full.
Not the suffering, intolerable, cruel,
Only the memory seared upon the soul
And the journey travelled long and hard
For one so young.
Now legs and feet are dextrous, strong,
Multi-talented,
But missing arms and hands replaced by science
Cannot replace the family
Killed and blown apart by war,
Nor cover for a young man's joy
Within the freedom of his body.
    We wait for words of bitterness, of rage,
But there are none;
Behind that slow, wise smile ~
Too old for teenage years ~
There lies no condemnation of the act,
No thought of fate's hard hand.
He who will never hold in naked tenderness,
But always must be held,
Speaks out his courage and his power,
Forgiveness and his strong resolve
'To work someday towards a lasting peace.'

Where Love Waits

Some think it morbid
To consider death
When life is in full flow.
This I cannot see:
Our death, as in our birth,
Encompasses a passing through
Into another world,
And the greater life, by far,
Exists beyond death's door.
How strange it is
That epitaphs seem carved
To pacify a world
That strives to hold all life
In earthly thrall.
But, that being so,
Perhaps I'll write my own
Knowing at least
The truth will then be shown ~
For I have lived
And known epiphanies,
Sere pain and ecstasy
Filling the chalice of my life,
And I have drunk of this wild wine
All-knowingly, seen the veil
Between the worlds lift and fade away
Leaving only radiancy and light.
And I have loved,
With all the depth and breadth
My heart could stand,
Knowing that love is all there is,
Above, about, around, below,
The only way to grow,
And, finally, to live.

Mea culpa ~ I have also sinned
Too much and need forgiving.
But, wounded, I have tried to cross the bridge
And taste of everything.
I know I shall return again
And, briefly as the mayfly,
Dance once more
Upon the waters of this life.
And so it is,
When time and fate see fit,
I'm eager, ready to depart,
Slipping through death's little door
To where Love waits.

A crystal horn ...

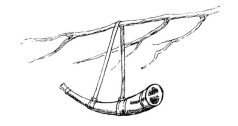

blown through the dark forests of the mind ...

In the clear moonlight the hunter raises the horn to his lips ~

a clarion call, echoing, reverberating through the woods,
across the countryside ...

the quarry leaps ahead ~

white and silver flashing through the trees ~

darting, evading, but, sometimes, captured, held.